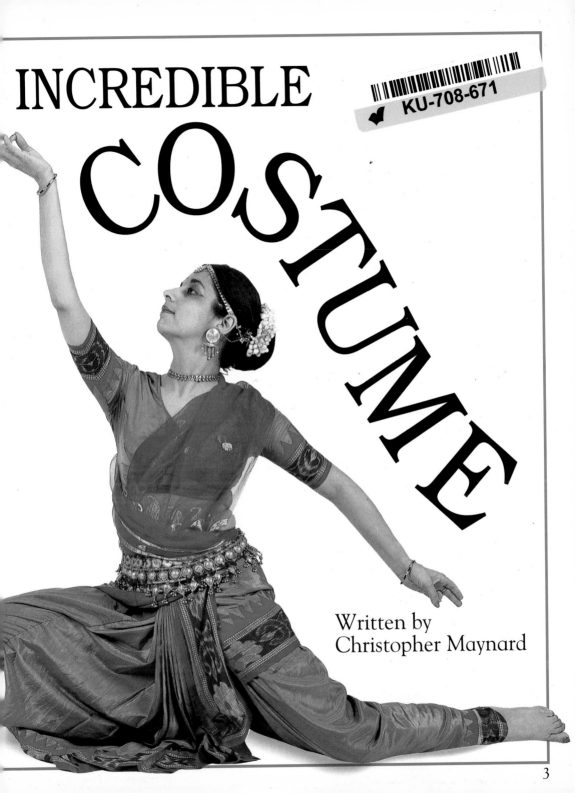

INCREDIBLE
COSTUME

Written by
Christopher Maynard

Contents

Second skin 6

The natural look 8

Under where? 10

Foot fads 12

Incredible cover-ups 14

Holding fast 16

Just the job 18

Safe suits 20

Fab fakes 22

Wonder wear 24

1970s platforms

4

SNAP SHOT™

Senior Editor
Mary Ling

Editor
Caroline Bingham

Art Editor
Joanna Pocock

Designer
Jane Thomas

Production
Catherine Semark

Consultant
Philip Wilkinson

A Dorling Kindersley Book

First published in Great Britain in 1995
by Snapshot™, an imprint of Covent Garden Books
9 Henrietta Street, London WC2E 8PS

Copyright © 1995 Covent Garden Books Limited, London
Photography by Peter Anderson, Andy Crawford,
Bob Gathany, Philip Gatward, Steve Gorton, Dave King,
Liz McAulay, Ray Moller, James Stevenson, Kim Taylor, Michael Zabé

Picture credits: British Museum/Nick Nicholls: 10tl;
The Image Bank/Daniel Hummel: 25bc; Royal Marines Museum: 25tl; Royal
Museum of Scotland: 7r; Tony Stone Worldwide/Robin Smith: 8tl/Charles
Thatcher: 18bl/Tony Stone: 18tr/David Bromley: 19r; Yorkshire Museum: 7tl.
All rights reserved.

Special thanks to: John Lewis Partnership, Shelly's Shoes, Park Beekeeping
Supplies, Cobra Sports Ltd., The Cricketers Club of London

Every effort has been made to trace the copyright holders
and we apologise in advance for any unintentional omissions. We
would be pleased to insert the appropriate acknowledgment in any
subsequent edition of this publication.

A CIP catalogue record for this book
is available from the British Library
ISBN 1-85948-036-5

Colour reproduction by Colourscan
Printed in Belgium by Proost

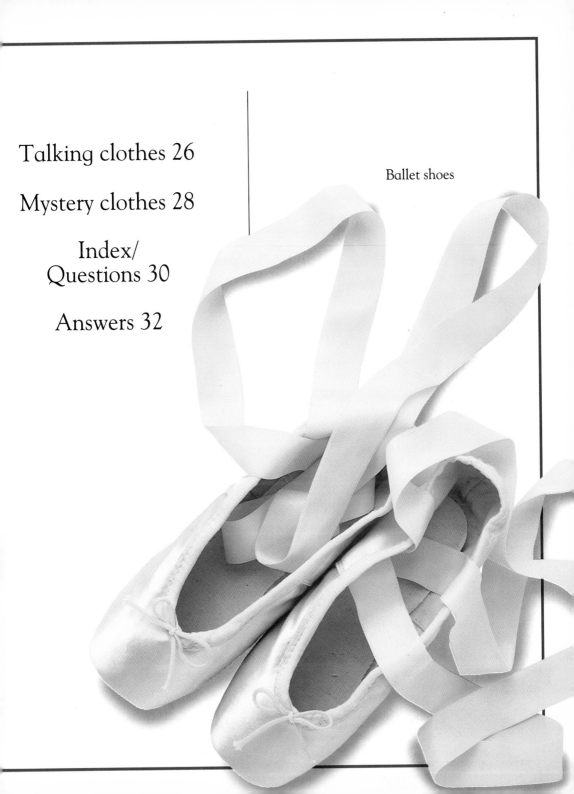

Talking clothes 26

Mystery clothes 28

Index/
Questions 30

Answers 32

Ballet shoes

Second skin

If human beings had furry hides it would be easy to run about naked. But we don't. Our clothes are like second skin that protects us from bitter cold, hot sun, and driving rain

Needle and thread

The invention of the needle meant skins could be sewn.

Hunters thought they took an animal's spi

A stone scrapes away fat to make the skin soft.

A flint knife separates the skin from the flesh.

The skin is "tanne to stop it rotting.

**Fi
fashic
Cave peo**
wore warm deersk
and other animal hic
with rough holes cut for t
head and arms to slip throug

Cloth kit

A simple upright loom was used to weave a length of cloth. The yarn was made from the wool of a sheep.

Loom

Clay or stone weights kept the threads hanging tightly.

Raw wool is made into yarn using a spindle.

by wearing its hide

Embroidered stories

With just a few stitches of yarn people decorated their clothes with amazing figures of the creatures they hunted and fished.

Spindle

Decorated Peruvian cloth

The natural look

Many clothes are made from plants. Some are even made with the help of a little worm!

The fluffy bolls of a cotton plant are spun into thread.

What plant can be turned

How a stripy T-shirt comes to be
Cotton fibres are spun and woven into cloth. This is dyed a bright colour, cut up, then sewn to make a T-shirt.

Denim jeans

Tough trousers
Denim is a hard-wearing, dyed cotton cloth. It was first made in the French town of Nîmes, so people called it "de Nîmes" – from which we get denim.

At the silk factory

Silk is a rich cloth made from the thread produced by silkworms. A silkworm caterpillar spins a cocoon of threads on a cluster of mulberry leaves.

Silkworm

The thread is produced from a hole under the silkworm's head.

Each cocoon is made of a thread more than half a mile long!

into a T-shirt or trousers?

Cotton T-shirt

Secret of the East

After its discovery in China almost 5,000 years ago, making silk became a secret guarded by the threat of death. It was used for majestic gowns worn by both men and women.

Japanese silk kimono

Light linens

The ancient Egyptians were the first to weave light, cool linen cloth from the fibres of the flax plant.

Under where?

When did you last change your underwear? Through the ages there have been many changes in style, from the comfortable to the bizarre.

This gymnast appears on an ancient Greek vase.

Gym bound

The first women to use bras were female gymnasts in ancient Greece. They wound material tightly around their chests to provide support.

The modern bra was invented in 1889

Hoops-a-daisy!

Imagine wearing a frame of steel hoops. A cage crinoline was worn to make dresses hang wide and full.

Bra business

Bras did not become really fashionable until about 75 years ago.

Modern-day bra with wire frame

The hoops were joined by bands of tape.

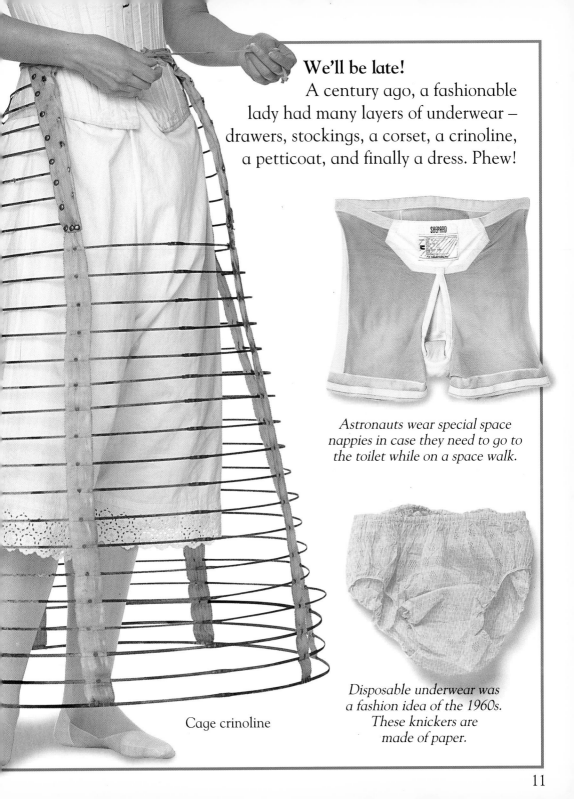

We'll be late!

A century ago, a fashionable lady had many layers of underwear – drawers, stockings, a corset, a crinoline, a petticoat, and finally a dress. Phew!

Astronauts wear special space nappies in case they need to go to the toilet while on a space walk.

Cage crinoline

Disposable underwear was a fashion idea of the 1960s. These knickers are made of paper.

Foot fads

No matter how strange they may look, shoes have only one purpos One way or another they have to protect the feet

Doctor's orders
Doc Marten first made protective, working boots known as DMs in 1967.

Stiletto

A lot of heel
Stilettos became popular 40 years ago. They are named after the narrow "stiletto" dagger, because of their pointed heels.

Some ancient Greek sandals had nails

Longfellows
In the 1300s, noblemen wore low-cut leather shoes with toes that could stretch up to 46 cm (18 in)!

These shoe flopped about as me walked, so their tips we tied to the ankle with core

opine

High as a kite

Platform shoes of the
1970s were nothing new.
In 10th-century Venice
the heels of shoes called
"chopines" reached a
towering 76 cm (30 in).

hese 1970s
atforms were
orn by a man.

n the soles that spelt out special messages

Fast forward

Trainers are designed for sports
such as basketball. Cushioned soles
protect the wearer's knees from
the violent jars they
receive.

Sports
shoe

*Most sports
shoes are held
on with laces.*

Incredible cover-ups

People have covered their heads for about 3,500 years. Originally hats were worn to protect against the weather, or to show authority, but they soon became essential fashion accessories too.

A knitted woollen hat keeps you warm.

In cold weather about 80% of your body

African head-dress

High time
A bright cotton or silk head-dress, known as a gele, is worn by West African women when they go to important celebrations.

Head gardener

This straw sun-hat is decorated with silk flowers and leaves, as if its wearer had fallen headlong into a garden border. It was high fashion 90 years ago, yet also gave lots of shade.

Straw hat

Hat city

Until the 1800s, the city of Fez in Morocco was the only place in the world where a stiff red felt hat with no brim was made.

...eat is lost from your head

A fez has a black tassel. ————

A gele is made from a large piece of material – about 1 m by 2 m (3 ft by 6 1/2 ft).

Moroccan fez

Holding fast

No matter how well made, most clothir sits badly on the body unless held in place. Braces, belts, elastic, and laces are just some of the fasteners we use

Velcro

Stick to me

After a walk in the country, Georges de Mestral noticed seeds with tiny hooks that stuck to his clothes. Velcro was based on this discovery.

A zip's teeth are set in a cloth tape.

Each tooth sits midway between teeth on the opposite side.

A metal or plastic slide forces the teeth to lock together as it advances.

Jaws

The zip was invented i America just over 100 years ago Early zips had big metal teeth and were used mainly for snowboots

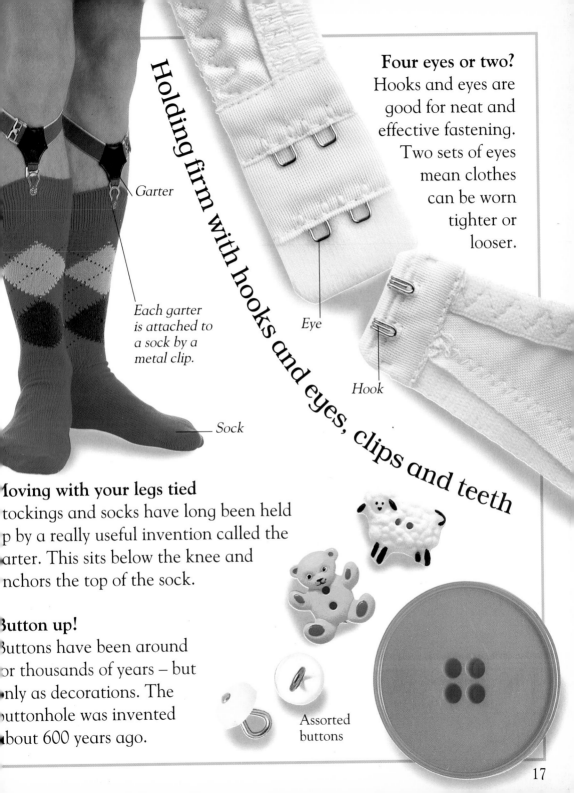

Holding firm with hooks and eyes, clips and teeth

Garter

Each garter is attached to a sock by a metal clip.

Sock

Four eyes or two?
Hooks and eyes are good for neat and effective fastening. Two sets of eyes mean clothes can be worn tighter or looser.

Eye

Hook

Moving with your legs tied

Stockings and socks have long been held up by a really useful invention called the garter. This sits below the knee and anchors the top of the sock.

Button up!

Buttons have been around for thousands of years – but only as decorations. The buttonhole was invented about 600 years ago.

Assorted buttons

Just the job

Can you spot a clown, a firefighter, and a chef? It's often easy to tell a person's job by what they wear.

Would anyone stop for a cop who dressed like a chef?

Sumo wrestler

Clown

Loin cloth

A sumo wrestler's nappy-lik loin cloth, huge apron, a topknot hairstyle are unchanged since the 1600s.

A clown's big nose and baggy clothes were invented by a clown of the 1860s.

The smell of grease paint

All clowns have their own special make-up and clothes, but they take the nickname "Joey" from a hugely popular clown called Joseph Grimal

Meltdown

Firefighters' clothes are all about safety. Their plastic helmets are fire-resistant, and their jackets and leggings are coated with a heavy plastic that won't burn or melt.

A French policeman

Long arm of the law

A gun on the hip, a badge, and a military style cap tell the world this man is a police officer.

Firefighter

A tall hat makes a chef stand out amidst all the bustle of a busy kitchen.

White heat

A chef's white uniform has to be cleaned frequently – or everyone will see the dirty stains! It is also cool to wear in a hot kitchen.

Chef

Safe suits

Whether under attack in
the boxing ring, or from
bees in the open air, special
clothes can help to protect the
wearer from serious damage.

RING PRO
AUSTRALIA

Bee wear

Beekeepers are rarely attacked – the
bees recognize them. But they always
wear protective
clothes.

*A veiled hat
keeps bees away
from the face
and head.*

*Tight sleeves stop
bees from crawling
up under clothing.*

*Smoke is puffed into
the hive to make
the bees drowsy.*

Extra padding

Boxers can be badly hurt
by a low blow. They wear
special padding to protec
their groin.

OZ /227 GR

Watch those hands

Boxers wear padded
gloves weighing up to
10 oz (280 g) to protect
their hands.

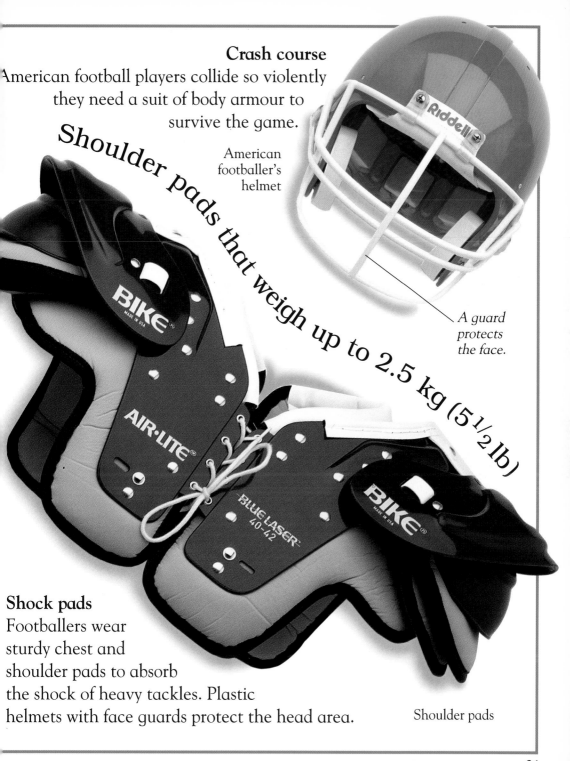

Crash course
American football players collide so violently they need a suit of body armour to survive the game.

American footballer's helmet

A guard protects the face.

Shoulder pads that weigh up to 2.5 kg (5 ½ lb)

BIKE MADE IN USA

AIR·LITE

BLUE LASER 40-42

BIKE MADE IN USA

Shock pads
Footballers wear sturdy chest and shoulder pads to absorb the shock of heavy tackles. Plastic helmets with face guards protect the head area.

Shoulder pads

Fab fakes

Fibres such as nylon and polyester come from oil, gas, and coal, and can copy the look and feel of cloth made of cotton and silk. They are sometimes mixed with natural fibres.

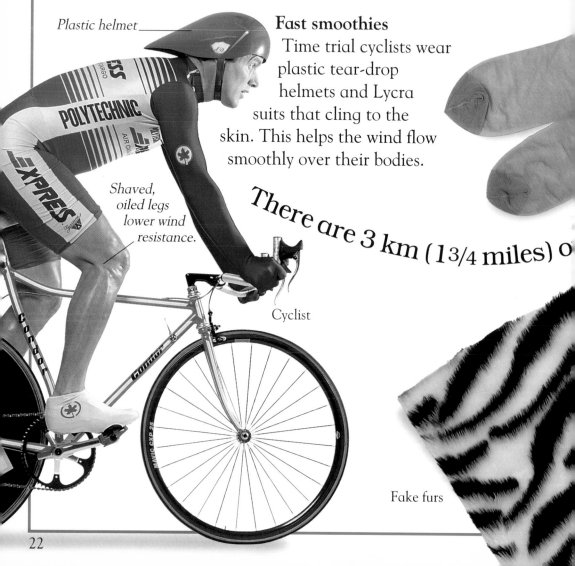

Plastic helmet

Fast smoothies
Time trial cyclists wear plastic tear-drop helmets and Lycra suits that cling to the skin. This helps the wind flow smoothly over their bodies.

Shaved, oiled legs lower wind resistance.

There are 3 km (1 3/4 miles) o

Cyclist

Fake furs

Nylon is a plastic that feels a bit like silk.

Nylon stockings

Stocking feat

Nylon was invented by Wallace H Carrothers in the late 1930s. Nylon made good stockings because of its strength and elasticity.

nylon thread in one nylon stocking

Fun fur

Fake fur costs much less than the real thing and it doesn't involve killing any wild animals.

Fake fur coat

Animal impersonators

Fake fibres can be dyed bright colours or marked to look like animal hide.

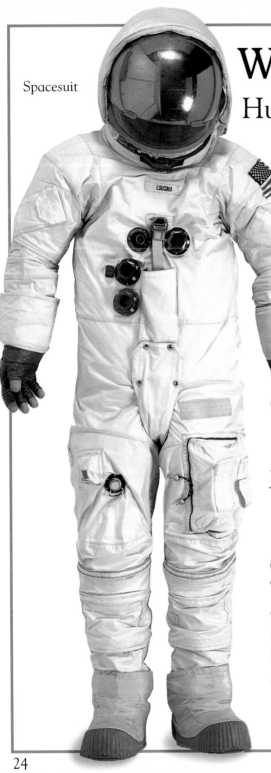

Spacesuit

Wonder wear

Humans can survive in ver
dangerous places – with
the right clothing.
Stripped of their suits
in space, astronauts'
blood would boil an
their bodies explode

Travelling light?
A spacesuit and backpack
weigh about 103 kg (227 lb),
but in space it's as light
as a feather.

From vacuum to freeze

Outer space wear
The spacesuit comes in two halves: a
of trousers and a jacket that snap
together. Gloves and helmet snap on
last. Water-cooled underwear keeps t
astronaut from over-heating.

Arctic
boots

Deep-sea danger
Deep-sea divers would
be crushed by water
pressure if not
protected by a
suit with a
hard shell.

*Hand-operated
grabbers*

Diving suit

Cold comforts
In the Arctic, at -40° C (-104° F)
and lower, feet can freeze in minutes.
Thick socks, lined boots, and
waterproof gaiters are
essential.

to oven ... the art of survival

Firefighter

*A hard glass
fibre pressure suit
encloses the diver's body.*

Hot too hot to handle
Firefighters sometimes
don synthetic suits
that let them work
in temperatures of
up to 170° C
(338° F) – as hot
as a kitchen
oven used for
baking cakes.

*A flush hood may be
worn if there is a danger
of chemicals exploding.*

*Heavy duty gloves
protect the hands.*

Talking clothes

Sometimes people put on special clothes that say they belong to a certain group, or they wear clothe to celebrate a special occasion.

You can see from the emblem on these ties that they are cricket club ties.

Keeping cool

This band of drummers wear the dress of a northern region of Ghana, West Africa. Loose tunics are cool in a hot climate.

West African drummers

Woven, narrov stripe clothes are typically wo. by Ghanaian me

For weddings

At western weddings, the bride is dressed in white (the same colour that the Chinese wear to funerals). In Jordan, the colour of a wedding dress is black.

An English bride in a silk dress and veil from the 1920s.

A bride from Palestine or Egypt wears a "desert veil".

1860s silk tartan dress

Wearing white can express sorrow or joy

Tartan tales

Tartans are worn by Highland Scots to show the clan or family they belong to. This silk tartan dress was worn by a small boy 130 years ago, when all children under the age of six wore dresses.

27

Mystery clothes

Some clothes have such strange shapes they don't look at all like what they are supposed to be. Here are five odd-looking pieces of clothing. Can you guess what each one is?

1. On what part of the body would people wear this bush?

2. Is this the cuff of a frilly shirt?

3. Would you wrap this around your neck?

4. This is not underwear, but it is worn under clothes. What is it?

5. Would you wear this to keep your hands or your feet warm?

Answers on page 32

Index

American footballer 21
Astronaut 24

Beekeeper 20
Boxer 20
Bra 10, 17
Button 17

Chef 19
Clown 18
Cotton 8

Deep-sea diver 25
Denim 8

Embroidery 7

Firefighter 19, 25
Fur
  animal 6
  fake 22, 23

Garter 17

Hats 14, 15

Linen 9
Loom 7

Nylon 23

Police officer 19
Polyester 23
Protective clothing 19, 20, 21, 24, 25

Silk 9
Shoes 12, 13
Stockings 23
Sumo wrestler 19

Tartan 27
Tie 26

Underwear 10, 11

Velcro 16

Weddings 27

Zip 16

Five well-dressed questions

1. What holds together with teeth?

2. Which shoes have hidden messages?

3. Before the invention of buttonholes, what were buttons used for?
  (a) wheels on very small carts
  (b) paying for food
  (c) as decoration on clothes

4. Which people love to dress up in tartans?

5. Which wrestlers wear nappies?

Answers on page 32

Who would have worn this scary costume?

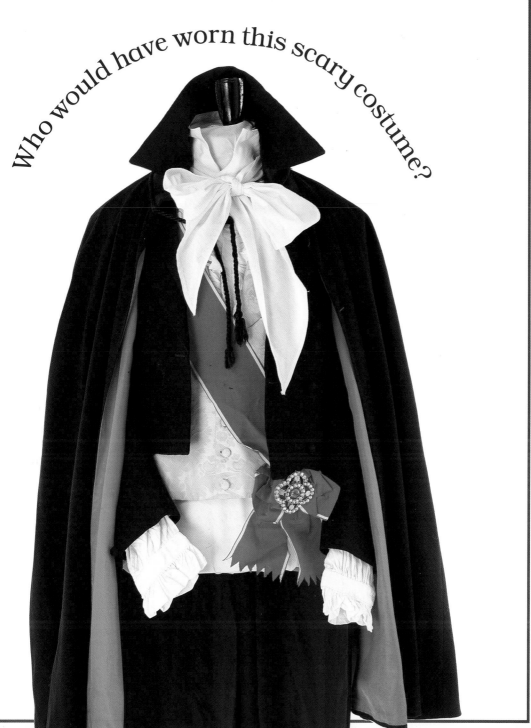

Answers

From page 28–29:   1. On your head – it's a hat

2. No, they are knickers from 1908

3. No, they are 1970s flared trousers

4. They are 18th-century pockets

5. Neither – it is a hat

From page 30:   1. A zip   4. The Scots

2. Ancient Greek sandals   5. Japanese sumo

3. As decoration on clothes   wrestlers

From page 31:   Dracula!